A Celtic Alphabet

FROM THE BOOK OF KELLS
AND OTHER SOURCES

Introduction by Dr A J Hughes

ANDREW WHITSON

First published in 1997 by
The Appletree Press Ltd, 19-21 Alfred Street,
Belfast, BT2 8DL
Tel: ++44 (0) 1232 243074
Fax: ++44(0) 1232 246756
email:frontdesk@appletree.ie
Copyright © Appletree Press, 1997

A Celtic Alphabet

A catalogue record for this book is available from The British Library.

website: www.irelandseye.com

ISBN 0 -86281-664-5

9 8 7 6 5 4 3 2 1

A Celtic Alphabet

FROM THE BOOK OF KELLS
AND OTHER SOURCES

Appletree Press

The 'Celtic Alphabets'

The title of this work has been carefully chosen.
It describes *A Celtic Alphabet,* simply because
it could be argued that there were many 'Celtic'
alphabets, or indeed that there were none!
If we look at the remains of Continental Celtic,
we can see that the Celts borrowed the alphabet
of their near neighbours. Thus in Spain, the
Celts borrowed an Iberian alphabet and adapted
it to their own language. In northern Italy,
inscriptions in the ancient Celtic language
known as Lepontic were written in an alphabet
borrowed from the Ligurians, while in ancient
Gaul, the Celtic inscriptions were written in
either Latin or Greek characters depending
on the area involved.

When we turn to Insular Celtic, and its two main branches of Goedelic (Irish, Manx and Scottish Gaelic) and Brittonic (Welsh, Cornish and Breton), we see that Latin is by far the common source for writing. Although the Christian church experienced extreme persecution in Rome at the time of Emperor Nero in the first century, by the time of Emperor Constantine, in the early fourth century, Christianity was accepted as an official religion. Latin was the language of the Roman Empire and was also the language of the early Christian church in western Europe. A Latin translation of the Bible (known as The Vulgate) was provided by Saint Jerome in the fourth century at the request of Pope Damasus and this text was central to Christian teaching in western Europe.

The adaptation of the Latin alphabet in Ireland

The year 432 is given as the traditional date for the arrival of Christianity in Ireland following the mission of Saint Patrick. Patrick, a Briton, spoke a British form of Celtic at home (which would be akin to modern Welsh or Cornish) but he wrote in Latin. Similarly, although he may have preached in Irish to the people of Ireland, he would have continued to write in Latin.

Most of the vocabulary relating to church buildings and ceremonies which exists in the Irish language today was borrowed from Latin in the fifth century: *cill* 'church', *easpag* 'bishop', *altóir* 'altar', *baisteadh* 'to baptise', which go back to Latin *cella, episcopus, altare, baptisare*. Eventually the Latin alphabet would also be adopted to write Old Irish, for while we have some Irish inscriptions (fourth-eighth centuries) in the Ogham script, a series of strokes and notches inscribed mainly on stone, it is believed that the inventor of this system of writing was also familiar with Latin.

The Irish or 'insular' script

The eminent Latin scholar and church historian, the late Ludwig Bieler, viewed the Irish script as 'a deliberate creation out of elements of several scripts inherited from antiquity which the earliest missionaries had brought with them'. Through time, the Irish monks themselves would become missionaries, not only to continental Europe but also to Scotland, a fine example being Donegal-born Saint Columba, or Columbkille (†597), who founded his famous monastery of Iona. From Iona, Irish missionaries would eventually make their way into northern England where they introduced this Irish, or insular style among the Anglo-Saxons in the seventh century. The later Carolingian reform saw the introduction of a new script in practically all of western Europe apart from

the Irish who maintained their 'insular script'. The English monk Bede, writing in the eighth century, also records that many English monks were educated in Ireland.

Illuminated manuscripts:
The Book of Durrow 650AD,
The Book of Kells 800AD

Between the late seventh and early ninth centuries, Irish monks produced illuminated manuscripts which were unrivalled in Europe for the exquisiteness of their art. The earliest surviving manuscript of any kind from Ireland is the *Cathach* or 'Battler', a psalm book written in Latin in the late sixth century. It is traditionally associated with Saint Columba (Columbkille) but this may or may not be true. One further significant feature of this manuscript is that we can trace to it the beginnings of the tradition of decorated capital letters. The *Cathach* would appear to have been influenced by the Coptic style, originating in Egypt, the place from where monasticism spread to Europe and, ultimately, Ireland. By the middle of the seventh century, Irish monks were perfecting a more ornate approach to the production of prestigious manuscripts most notably in the *Book of Durrow,* 650 AD, the earliest extant example of such a manuscript, in a highly artistic style which would culminate in the magnificent *Book of Kells,* dated by most scholars to around the year 800. Both these books are named after Irish midland monasteries: Durrow, County Laois, and Kells, County Meath, and both are now housed in Trinity College, Dublin.

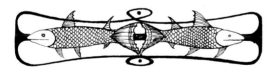

As regards the *Book of Kells,* however, the Columban community came to Kells in 806, having left the Scottish island of Iona due to Viking

raids, and it may well be that the *Book of Kells* was begun, or even produced, on Iona, and it is also thought that the *Book of Durrow* may have been originated in Iona, or even Northumbria. Other artistic books of this type were undertaken in Ireland at this period, although many have not survived. The Welsh-born Anglo-Norman monk Giraldus Cambrensis who visited Kildare in 1187 described an illuminated manuscript "so delicate and subtle, so exact and compact, so full of knots and links, with colours so fresh and vivid, that you might say that all this was the work of an angel and not of a man".

Although these books are best described as Celtic manuscripts due to their art form, their contents were Christian. Both the Books of Durrow and Kells contain texts from the Gospel, but it has been justly remarked that these manuscripts allowed pre-Christian Celtic art an exciting new medium to express itself in the form of vellum manuscript.

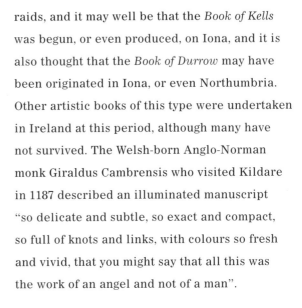

The tools of the trade

Clive Thomas, in his book *Celtic Britain,* has
described the act of writing in Europe as
essentially a Latin-based craft, and it is hardly
surprising that both the Irish word *peann* and the
English word *pen* both go back to Latin *penna*
which means 'feather, or quill'. The main writing
tool was a goose-quill, or a crow-quill for fine
work. It is clear that the Irish-speaking scribes,
who produced manuscripts both in Latin and in
Irish, were also heavily influenced by Latin in
their choice of other words associated with
writing, such as: *leabhar* 'a book', *litir* 'a letter',
líne 'a line', *scríobh* 'to write' etc, all borrowed
from Latin *penna, liber, littera, linea* and *scribere.*

The main material on which the manuscripts
were produced was vellum, or calf-skin,

as opposed to papyrus 'paper'. It may have taken vellum from a herd of up to 150 calves to produce the *Book of Kells!* Ink was vegetable based, made from oak-galls, and manuscripts produced in Ireland were renowned for the durable black quality of their ink - indeed the Irish term for ink *dúch,* literally 'blackener', is one of the few native Irish terms associated with writing based on the word *dubh* 'black'.

Dyes were also used to provide a variety of other colours and included the north European plants woad and indigo, while minerals were also used such as copper-based verdigris, red and white lead, and the precious blue stone lapis lazuli, a lucrative Afghanistan import from the Himalayas. In the *Book of Kells* kermes was used, a material produced from the body of a pregnant Mediterranean insect. No gold was used and orpiment (yellow arsenic sulphide) was used as an alternative to gold.

Most of the early monasteries had a special building set aside for the purposes of writing called a *scriptorium.* Many of the manuscripts were kept in a satchel (known in Old Irish *tíag* borrowed from Greek *theca*). Some of the later manuscripts had a special shrine, or *cumhdach.* These shrines were manufactured from wood, metal and precious stones. Sometimes the shrines were built in periods later than the original manuscripts. Examples of these shrines have survived, such as those for the Stowe Missal, a Latin Mass-book of the early Irish church produced in 800, although the shrine probably dates to 1050. Owing to the popular (but unproven) belief that the *Book of Durrow* had been copied by Saint Columbkille, Flann mac Sechnaill (†916), the king of Ireland, had an elaborate shrine made for it, a shrine lost from the library in Trinity College Dublin in the late seventeenth century. This custom of enshrining manuscripts in elaborate casks continued when

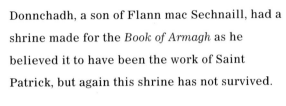

Donnchadh, a son of Flann mac Sechnaill, had a shrine made for the *Book of Armagh* as he believed it to have been the work of Saint Patrick, but again this shrine has not survived.

The preservation of the great gospel books may be due to the fact that they were looked upon as relics. An Irish text of 1007 described the *Book of Kells* as 'the great Gospel of Colum Cille, the chief relic of the Western World'. We know, for instance, that the *Cathach* was actually carried into battle as a talisman by the O'Donnells, and a similar use was made by others of the *Book of Armagh* until its capture in the twelfth century by Anglo-Norman John de Courcy, who later returned it. Some uses of manuscripts as relics with special powers were more detrimental than others, as in the case of the *Book of Durrow* which was apparently dipped in water in the seventeenth century as a cure for cattle. While the fate of the beasts is not known, the immersion process caused stain damage to the manuscript.

Celtic Art style

While the texts of these illuminated manuscripts can be firmly dated to the era of Christianity in Ireland, the form of decoration and native artwork was drawn from earlier Iron Age Celtic art work, especially spiral designs. Animal ornament of fantastic complexity can be seen to incorporate influences from Germanic lands, while the intricate ribbon interlace can be traced to Mediterranean and Near East influences. Some of the 'carpet' pages in the *Book of Durrow* bear a striking resemblance to objects found in the early sixth century grave of an East Anglian nobleman at Sutton Hoo. The *Book of Kells,* the Hiberno-Latin illuminated manuscript par excellence shows similarities to Byzantine, Greek and Coptic styles. Even the treatment of vellum was given a particular Irish

flavour, as suede-surfaced insular vellum was used in the *Book of Durrow,* as opposed to the smoother continental vellum, and this *Durrow* technique proved stunningly receptive to both ink and colours.

The visual can always express art style much more immediately than the written word and Appletree Press offers an interpretation of this art style in the pages which follow. However, if you are interested in detailed treatment of the art of this period, you may wish to consult some of the volumes listed below.

Further Reading

Ruth & Vincent Megaw
Celtic Art from its beginnings to the Book of Kells
(THAMES & HUDSON, LONDON 1989)

P Brown
The Book of Kells: Forty-eight Pages and Details
(THAMES AND HUDSON, LONDON 1995)

G Henderson
From Durrow to Kells: The Insular Gospel, Books 650-800
(THAMES AND HUDSON, LONDON 1987)

Iain Bain
Celtic Knotwork
(CONSTABLE, LONDON 1986)

Timothy O'Neill
The Irish Hand: Scribes and their Manuscripts from the earliest times to the seventeenth century with an exemplar of Irish scripts, with an
Introduction by F J Byrne
(THE DOLMEN PRESS, DUBLIN 1984)

Bb

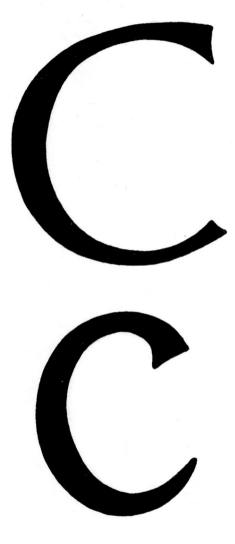

Ee

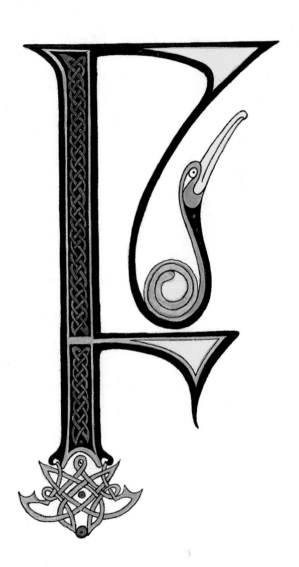

Gg

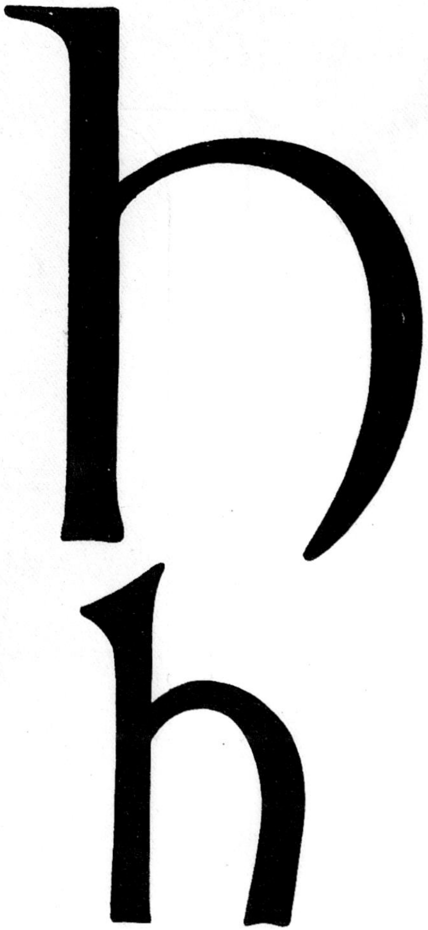

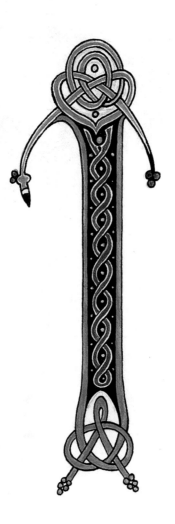

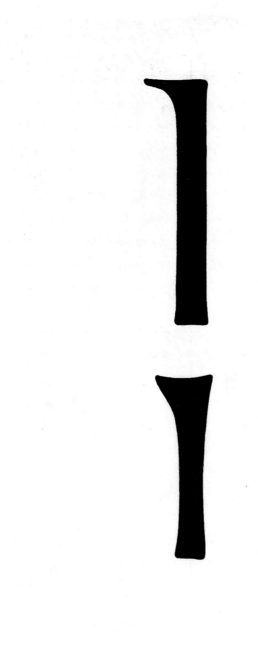

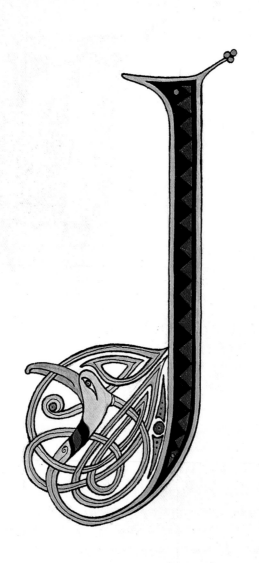

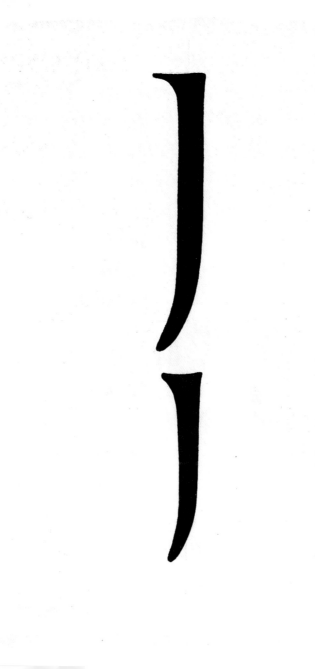

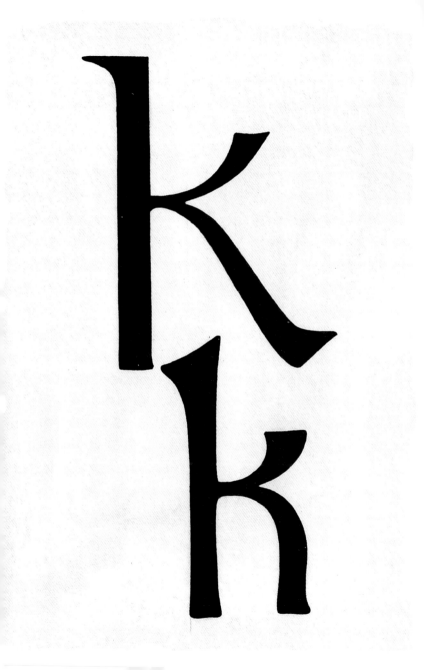

N n

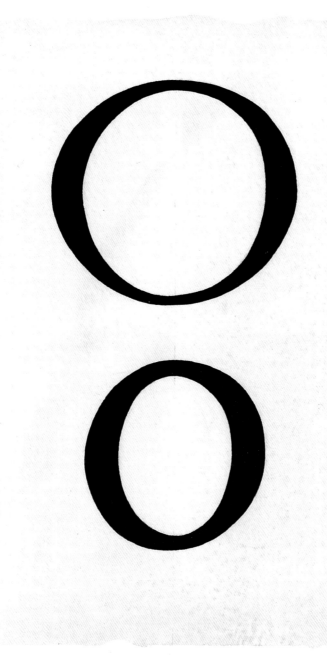

R

R

S s

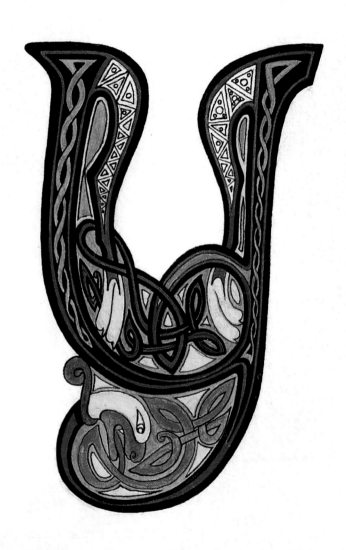

Yy

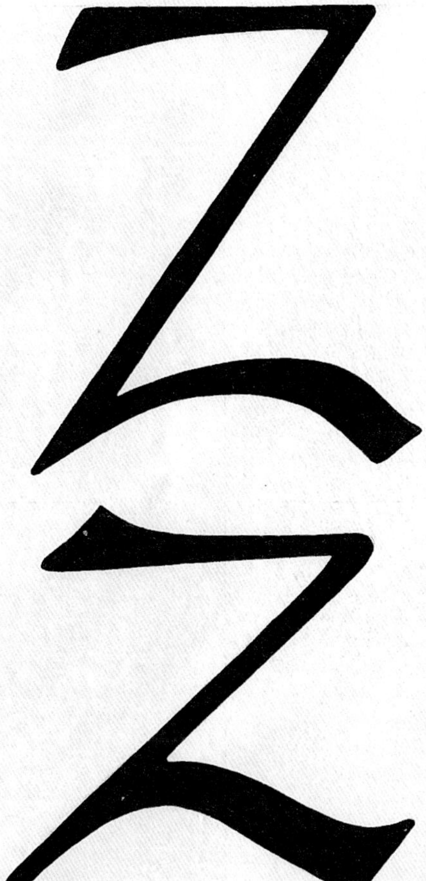